The Joy Luck Club

Club

Amy Tan

TEACHER GUIDE

NOTE:

The trade book edition of the novel used to prepare this guide is found in the Novel Units catalog and on the Novel Units website. Using other editions may have varied page references.

Please note: We have assigned Interest Levels based on our knowledge of the themes and ideas of the books included in the Novel Units sets, however, please assess the appropriateness of this novel or trade book for the age level and maturity of your students prior to reading with them. You know your students best!

ISBN 978-1-56137-894-4

To order, contact your
local school supply store, or:

Toll-Free Fax: 877.716.7272
Phone: 888.650.4224
3901 Union Blvd., Suite 155
St. Louis, MO 63115

sales@novelunits.com

novelunits.com

Table of Contents

Plot Summary 3

About the Author 3

Background Information 4

Initiating Activities 5

Predictions, Anticipation Guide, Pre-Reading Discussion, Book Hook,
Response Logs, Role Play, Writing, Brainstorming, Novel Sleuth

Vocabulary Activities 9

Vocabulary, Discussion, Writing Ideas, Activities

Feathers From a Thousand *Li* Away

Jing-mei Woo: The Joy Luck Club 11

An-mei Hsu: Scar 12

Lindo Jong: The Red Candle 14

Ying-ying St. Clair: The Moon Lady 15

The Twenty-Six Malignant Gates

Waverly Jong: Rules of the Game 17

Lena St. Clair: The Voice from the Wall 18

Rose Hsu Jordan: Half and Half 20

Jing-mei Woo: Two Kinds 21

American Translation

Lena St. Clair: Rice Husband 23

Waverly Jong: Four Directions 25

Rose Hsu Jordan: Without Wood 27

Jing-mei Woo: Best Quality 28

Queen Mother of the Western Skies

An-mei Hsu: Magpies 30

Ying-ying St. Clair: Waiting Between the Trees 31

Lindo Jong: Double Face 32

Jing-mei Woo: A Pair of Tickets 34

Post-reading Questions for Discussion or Writing 36

Post-reading Activities 37

Summary

The Joy Luck Club is actually a story collection—a four-part set of sixteen interlocking stories about four Chinese-American daughters and their four native-born mothers. The four older women are friends—members of the "Joy Luck Club"—a group of mah jong players that has been meeting in San Francisco since 1949. The tales, each told in the first-person, reveal the loving—but tension-fraught—relationships of mothers and daughters who grew up in different cultures.

About the Author

Amy Tan was born in Oakland, California, in 1952 to John Tan (1914-1968) and Daisy Tan (1916-). She has a brother, a half-brother, and three half-sisters; another brother died at age 17, the year before the death of her father. She graduated from high school in Switzerland (Montreux, 1969) and went on to earn her B. A. and her master's degree in Linguistics from San José State University.

She has worked at a variety of jobs, including: switchboard operator, A&W carhop, Round Table bartender and pizza maker, Language Development Consultant to programs for developmentally-disabled children, copywriter for a medical education newsletter, and freelance business writer specializing in telecommunications.

The Joy Luck Club was her first published book (1989) and has been made into a major motion picture (1994) in which she makes a cameo appearance. She has been married since 1974 to Lou DeMattei and currently lives in San Francisco with her husband, her cat, Sagwa, and her dog, Mr. Zo. They have no children.

Her contact address is that of her agent: Sandra Dijkstra, 1155 Camino del Mar, Del Mar, CA 92014.

Other books by Amy Tan:

The Kitchen God's Wife
The Hundred Secret Senses
The Moon Lady and *The Chinese Siamese Cat*—children's books

Background Information

After the Opium War, the Treaty of Nanking forced China to open Shanghai and four other ports to overseas trade. The International Colony and the French Concession arose, and Shanghai grew quite "western" in appearance. The Communist party was founded in Shanghai in 1921. Students and workers, however, generally supported the Nationalist Party (Kuomintang), founded by Sun Yat-sen in 1911 and led after 1925 by Chiang Kai-shek. It was the dominant party in mainland China until 1948.

Taiwan, or "Nationalist China," is an island separated from the southeast coast of China by the Formosa Strait. It was a possession of Japan between 1895 and 1945. Fifteen percent of the population are members of the Kuomintang party who escaped China after the country fell to the Communists in 1949. The Xindang Party insists on the unification of China and Taiwan, while the Kuomintang and Minjindang parties both want recognition of independence.

After war was declared between Japan and the U.S., the Japanese occupied foreign concessions in China. Japan capitulated, but terrible living conditions persisted until Communist troops reached Shanghai in 1949.

Terms to Know

Taoism—the philosophical system evolved by Lao-tzu and Chuang-tzu, advocating a life of complete simplicity and naturalness and of non-interference with the course of natural events, in order to attain a happy existence in harmony with the Tao

Confucian—a believer in the doctrines of Confucius, a philosopher and teacher who codified the traditional Chinese principles of ethics, morals, and politics in a series of well-known sayings

Buddhism—a relatively late addition to Chinese traditions, a religion that originated in India, holding that life is full of suffering caused by desire and that the way to end this suffering is through enlightenment that allows one to stop the otherwise endless cycle of births and deaths

Initiating Activities

1. **Prediction:** Have students examine the cover illustration and title, then flip through the book. **Ask:** What kind of book do you suppose this will be? When and where will it be set? How many students have seen the movie?

2. **Anticipation Guide:** Present students with these statements and have them discuss whether they agree or disagree—and why.
    a) Life is largely a matter of luck and fate.
    b) The relationship between a mother and daughter is special.
    c) Children owe their parents something.
    d) I believe in certain superstitions.
    e) Crying is manipulative.
    f) You should listen to your mother.
    g) It is important to know about your ancestry.
    h) Memories are stories, not truths.
    i) You should swallow your tears.
    j) Most mothers are martyrs.
    k) The more choices you have in life, the better.
    l) Losing face is one of the worst things that can happen to you.
    m) The most important thing is to be true to yourself.
    n) Consideration for others should guide your actions.
    o) There has to be equality in a good marriage.
    p) Opposites attract.
    q) A marriage without love is no good.

3. **Pre-reading Discussion Topics and Questions:**

    Immigrants—What are some of the reasons people have for emigrating to the United States? What are some problems they encounter here? What misunderstandings sometimes arise between immigrant parents and their children? What do you know about the experiences of Chinese immigrants, in particular? What does it mean to "be an American"? Do you think it is important to know about your heritage? Why or why not?

    Mothers and Daughters—Do you think mothers and daughters have a special bond? Do mothers expect different things from daughters than from sons? What are some typical mother-daughter conflicts? What are some of the "double binds" mothers might put their daughters in? and vice versa? How would you define a "good mother"? a "good daughter"? What's hard about being a "good mother"? What's difficult about being a "good daughter"?

Story-telling—Why do people enjoy telling and listening to stories? Where do you find storytelling situations, today? Do teenagers ever sit around and tell stories? What kind? Do men and women participate in "gossip" equally?

China—What happened to China during World War II? Who were the Kuomintang? What happened when the Japanese invaded? What do you know about Taoism? Confucianism? Buddhism?

4. **"Book Hook"**: To generate interest in the book, read the description of how June Woo's mother began the Joy Luck Club in China during World War II—pp. 9-12, "I thought up Joy Luck on a summer night...And that's how we came to call our little parties Joy Luck."

5. **Log:** Have students keep a response log as they read.

    (a) In one type of log, the student pretends to be one of the characters. For example, for stories told by the mothers, students could pretend to be the daughters. Writing on one side of each piece of paper, the student writes in the first person ("I...") about his/her reactions to what happened in that chapter. A partner (or the teacher) responds to these writings on the other side of the paper.

    (b) In the dual entry log, students jot down brief summaries and reactions to each section of the novel they have read. (The first entry could be made based on a preview of the novel—a glance at the cover and a flip through the book.)

Pages	Summary	Reactions
		(For example: "This reminded me of the time...," "June's mother reminds me of...," "If I were Waverly...," "I disagree with Lena's mother when she says...")

    (c) In a third type of log, students choose a passage from each section that strikes them for some reason, copy it—and explain why the passage seems important to them. Has the author used language in a special way? created beautiful word pictures? expressed an important insight? raised a question in the student's mind? somehow reminded the student of something in his or her own life?

(d) In a fourth type of log, students divide the page into three columns and respond to the story in three ways:
- comments/questions for the characters
- comments/questions for the author
- comments about the reader's personal reactions to the story

(e) As an alternative to keeping a separate journal, as students read they might simply jot thoughts and questions on sticky notes and apply them to the relevant passage in question for later reference during literature circle discussion.

6. **Role Play:** Have groups of students improvise skits showing the following situations (like situations in the book). After they meet the analogous situation in the story, they should discuss how it compares with their improvisation.
   - A mother and daughter are shopping in the mall when the mother runs into one of her friends and begins bragging about the daughter's accomplishments. The daughter is irritated and embarrassed—especially since the mother has exaggerated her talents…
   - A daughter has returned home from college for Thanksgiving break. Her mother wastes no time criticizing her weight, her clothes, her boyfriend…
   - A young professional couple are speaking to a marriage counselor. It turns out that both the husband and the wife have a litany of complaints...

7. **Writing:** Have students freewrite for ten minutes using one of the following "starters."
   Mothers and daughters…
   Having immigrant parents…
   Knowing about your heritage…
   In China before 1949, a woman…

8. **Brainstorming:** Have students free-associate with the phrase "to be an American." Write the phrase on the board. For ten minutes or so, have students share anything that comes to mind when they hear that phrase. Jot their responses around the phrase, organizing them into categories such as laws of citizenship, "American" culture, first/second generation, etc.

See the next page for a suggested framework.

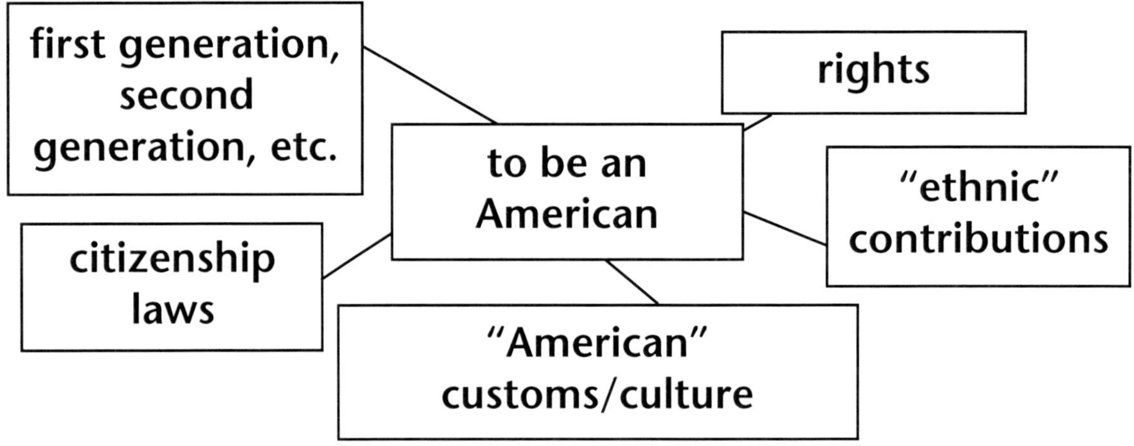

9. **Novel Sleuth:** Instruct students to look as they read for instances of mother-daughter conflict (to be marked "MDC") and instances of culture clash (to be marked CC). Students will refer back to these details when discussing and writing about the themes of tradition and change. (Use removable sticky notes.)

   Also have students mark examples of making choices (CH+) and failing to make choices (CH–). Students will refer to these details when discussing and writing about the themes of fate and faith in *The Joy Luck Club.*

10. As they read, have students fill in a graphic organizer like the one below as they read to help them remember "who's who." In the square for each name, they should list memorable details/descriptors. They should label each arrow with a brief description of the relationship. (See Student Packet, Activity #3, for a larger reproducible of this activity.)

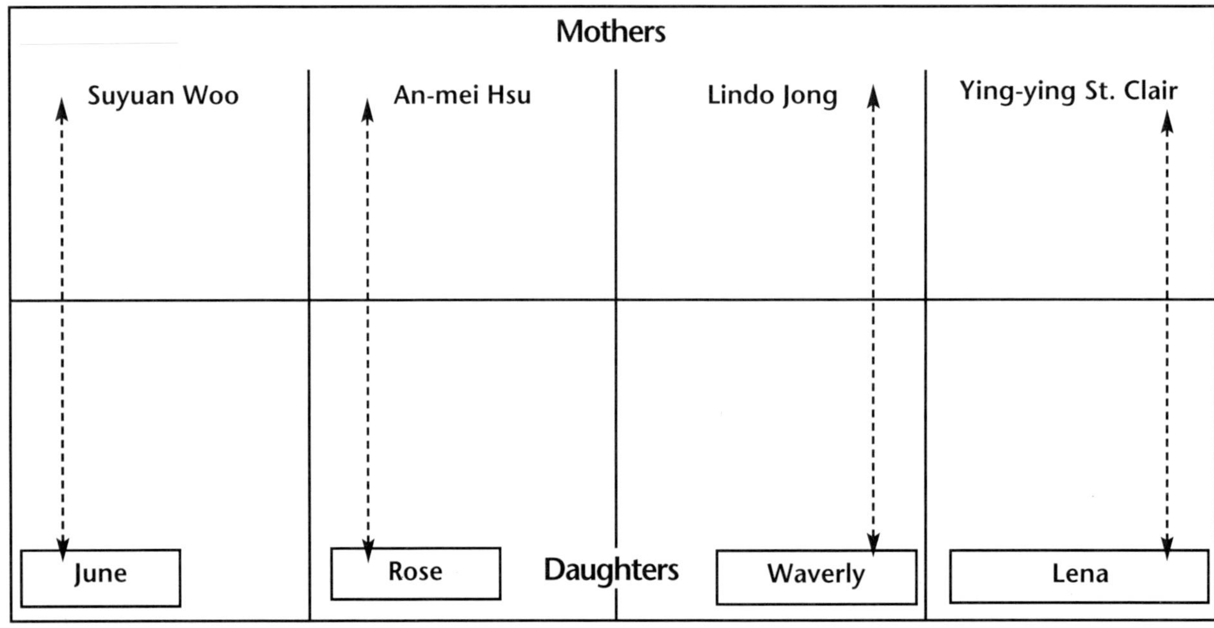

Vocabulary Activities

(Note: Also see the reproducibles in the student packet for this title.)

1. Introduce students to the vocabulary words found in this guide's vocabulary lists. Before students read a particular section of the book, pronounce the selected vocabulary words for that section. As students read the story, have them fill out a chart like the following. After reading the word in context, they should predict the definition and discuss the context clues they used to arrive at their guesses. Finally, they should jot down the dictionary definition that fits the way the word is used in the book.

Word	Page	Prediction	Dictionary Definition

2. As an alternative to Activity #1, have students keep a running list of words in the story that are unfamiliar to them. Instruct them to write down what they think each word means, from its context—and why. Then they should consult a dictionary and jot down the appropriate definition.

Word	Page	What I Think It Means	Clues I Used	Dictionary Definition

3. After students have read the novel, have them pick the ten words they believe it is most important to know in order to understand the book—and ask them to tell why.

4. Have students "map" selected words that fit into the following framework:

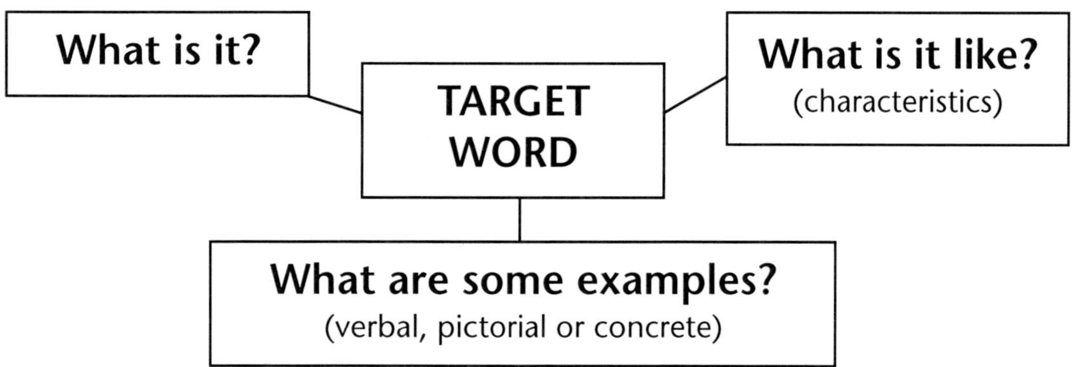

A map for "cicadas" (page 43) might look like this:

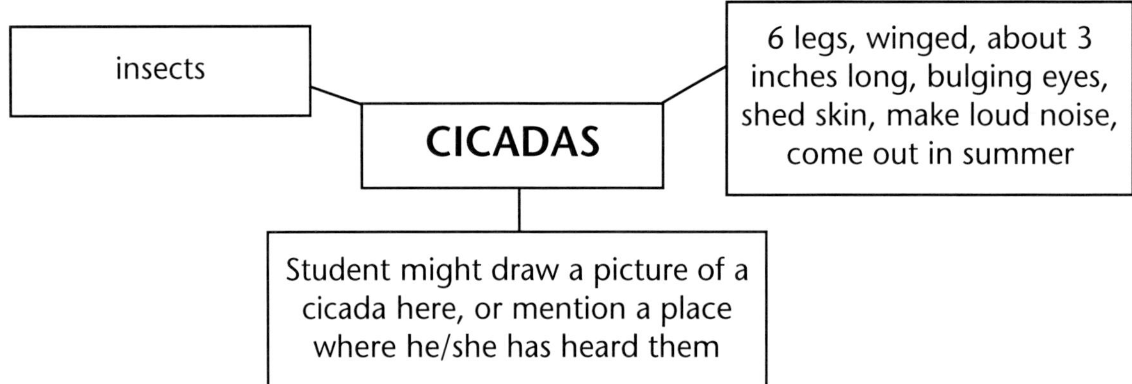

Words students might map this way: *mah jong (5), candelabra (16), settee (37), palanquin (52), gingko (73, prawns (91), benefactor (94), prodigy (99), armoire (159), omens (159), sham (169), trellis (174), foyer (214), refuge (218), carcasses (232), lute (264), pagoda (266), spouse (302), scaffolding (317), itinerary (318), hoisin sauce (320), surname (322), missionary (326)*

5. Before students read the book, have them sort words in the box below into the following categories: **people, food, places, furniture, human qualities (positive and negative).**

   Students might work individually on their guesses, then break into groups to discuss their choices. Using dictionaries, each group should come up with a final sorting upon which everyone agrees. The whole class could then convene to discuss any differences in opinion among groups—especially concerning whether particular human qualities are positive or negative.

Mandarin (17)	wonton (18)	cilantro (20)	oblivious (26)
concubines (35)	insolent (36)	settee (37	compound (45)
lacquer (49)	amah (65)	pavilion (73)	gingko (73)
brigands (78)	wantonness (81)	dim sum (90)	prawns (91)
adversaries (95)	benevolently (97)	humility (97)	phlegmy (99)
brashness (123)	regal (135)	sulky (150)	remorse (165)
anorexic (166)	manipulative (179)	puritanical (193)	amorous (198)
foyer (214)	obsessively (214)	despicable (217)	refuge (218)
tofu (236)	pagoda (266)	longevity (293)	spouse (302)
sheepish (318)	forlorn (320)	missionary (326)	

Vocabulary • Discussion
Writing Ideas • Activities

Feathers from a Thousand *Li* Away

All four of these stories are about the mothers' successes and failures at conveying their heritage to their daughters.

Jing-mei Woo: The Joy Luck Club—pages 3-32

The first story opens shortly after the death of one of the mothers (Suyuan Woo); her daughter, Jing-mei (June), has taken her place at the mah jong table. Jing-mei soon learns that the other three women want her to go to China, visit the two half-sisters she has never met, and tell them about their recently-deceased mother.

Vocabulary

mah jong 5	aneurysm 5	gruel 12	nondescript 15
tweed 16	candelabra 16	Mandarin 17	wonton 18
copywriter 20	cilantro 20	camphor 21	translucent 21
recoup 26	oblivious 26	guise 28	

Discussion Questions

1. What is the old woman's memory about the swan (p. 3)? (They sailed across the ocean together, but immigration officials took the swan.) Why hasn't she given her daughter the feather? (She's waiting to perfect her English.) Will she? What tone does this opening piece establish? (magical) How is it related to the first story in the book (p. 5)? (June's mother also sailed across the ocean.)

2. What are your impressions of Jing-mei's mother? (died recently; sociable— began the Joy Luck Club; plucky—lost everything in the war) How do you form these impressions of what she was like? (Jing-mei's story and her mother's stories)

3. What are your impressions of Jing-mei? (articulate, sensitive, thinks her mother was too critical) Is she like anyone you know? Is she like you in any way? Do you know anyone who, like her, has dealt with bilingualism? What would it be like to talk to your parents in English and have them respond in another language?

4. Why have Jing-mei and the others gathered at the Hsus' house? (The men play cards, the women play mah jong.) How does Jing-mei seem to feel about taking her mother's place? (uncomfortable) How would you feel?

5. What can you tell about the relationship Jing-mei had with her mother? What does she mean when she says she never understood her mother? (They didn't "speak the same language"—literally and figuratively.) How does she seem to feel about her mother's death? (sad, confused)

6. How did the original Joy Luck Club start in China? (June's mother organized mah jong parties with three other friends to escape the horrors of war.) How did the San Francisco version begin? (She began a San Francisco version with women she met at church when she moved there in 1949.) Why was that name chosen for it? (Their only joy was the hope of good luck.) Why do you suppose that name was also given to the group in San Francisco?

7. Why did Jing-mei's mother go to Kweilin during the war? (Her husband thought she would be safe there.) How did it "lose its beauty" for her? (She saw death and misery there.) Did she seem bitter about her experiences there? (yes) Why do you suppose she told the story over and over?

8. What sorts of stories did Jing-mei's mother and her friends tell at their weekly parties? (funny ones) Was it wrong for them to laugh when surrounded by so much misery? Can you think of other examples of this sort of "coping mechanism"?

9. How was the new Joy Luck Club like the old one? (four women friends) How was it different? (not in the midst of war; also an investment club) How do you picture Jing-mei's mother? Auntie Lin? Auntie Ying? Auntie An-mei? How can people be "both best friends and arch enemies" (p. 27)?

10. Why have the women given June a check? (to buy a plane ticket to China) Why do they want her to go? (to meet her sisters and tell them about their mother) How does she feel about going? (unsure of herself and what she will say) **Prediction:** What do you think happened to the twin babies?

Writing Idea: Imagine that you are in June's position—going off to meet some half-sisters you have never seen, trying to describe your mother to them. Write the description of your mother that you would share.

An-mei Hsu: Scar—pages 33-41

The second story is told by one of the mothers, An-mei Hsu. After An-mei's mother disgraced the family by becoming a concubine, An-mei and her brother were raised by their grandmother (Popo) and an aunt. One day their mother appeared at dinnertime. In the confusion, An-mei was badly scalded by a pot of soup. The mother returned years later when Popo lay on her deathbed; An-mei came to love her as she watched her try to cure Popo by cutting a piece of flesh from her own arm.

Vocabulary

dowry 35   concubines 35   insolent 36   settee 37

Discussion Questions

1. Why did An-mei's grandmother refer to her mother as a "ghost"? What does she mean, "To say her name is to spit on your father's grave" (p. 34)? (She disgraced her family by becoming a concubine.) Why do you suppose An-mei's mother became a concubine?

2. How did An-mei get along with her grandmother? (feared but loved her) with her aunt? (They didn't waste affection on each other.) Why did Popo tell so many frightening stories? (to teach An-mei to behave) Why do you think Auntie treated An-mei and her brother so harshly?

3. Why do you think An-mei's mother left her children with Popo? (Popo wouldn't let the children go.) Did they feel abandoned? Resentful? (no—confused)

4. What is "shou"? (filial respect) What values does Popo want An-mei to have? (respect for family and tradition; submission and obedience)

5. How did An-mei receive the scar under her chin? (She was badly burned by soup.) Why do you suppose the chapter is entitled "scar"? What is the symbolic significance of the scar? (An-mei's mother's shame scarred An-mei's life.)

6. How did Popo care for An-mei while she was sick? (She poured soothing water on the wound, peeled the scab.) Why did her mother leave? (Popo drove her away.) Why did Popo talk to An-mei about her small funeral? (so she wouldn't give up and die) Do you think An-mei would have died without Popo's care?

7. What does An-mei mean when she says that the woman she worshiped was not the same woman who came to Popo's deathbed (p. 40)? What is she saying about memories? (They are a combination of fact and creativity.)

8. Why do you think An-mei's mother came back when Popo was dying? Would Popo have ordered her away if she had been lucid? (probably)

9. Why did An-mei's mother cut her own arm? (She was engaging in ritual, trying to cure her mother.) What does An-mei mean when she says, "Even though I was young, I could see the pain of the flesh and the worth of the pain"? (She understood her mother's respectful, devoted actions even then.)

10. Do you think An-mei's mother and Popo loved each other? What sort of mother do you suppose Popo was to An-mei's mother as she was growing up?
    Prediction: Who do you think raised An-mei after Popo died?

Writing Idea: Popo tells many stories to teach her grandchildren lessons about greed, listening to one's elders, etc. Find a contemporary children's story that teaches a lesson and summarize the story. Analyze the values the story promotes.

Lindo Jong: The Red Candle—pages 42-63

The third story is told by Lindo Jong ("Auntie Lin")—apparently to her daughter, Waverly. Promised in marriage at age two to a bossy, self-centered boy, Lindo was taken from her family when she was twelve. For the next few years, she was treated as a servant; the wedding was held when she was sixteen. A servant was supposed to watch a candle during the night to make sure that it did not go out, but Lindo blew it out when the servant left the room. Unhappy in her marriage to Tyan-yu, Lindo came up with a plan for escaping from it. She convinced her mother-in-law, who was eager for a grandchild, that a dream had revealed to her that a pregnant servant was carrying Tyan-yu's child. The family gave Lindo enough money to go to America.

Vocabulary

cicadas 43	betrothed 44	compound 45	pretense 49
lacquer 49	prestige 49	felicitous 52	palanquin 52
auspicious 59	imperial 62		

Discussion Questions

1. What was the contrast between the marriage in the war movie and Lindo's first marriage? (The soldier goes home and marries someone he will stay with forever; Lindo's marriage didn't last.) How and why did Lindo make a sacrifice for her family? (She agreed to an arranged marriage because it was expected of her.)
2. Why is this chapter called "The Red Candle"? (The candle was supposed to be kept lighted throughout the wedding night to ensure the marriage bond was unbreakable.) Why did Lindo blow out the candle? (She wanted the marriage to end.)
3. Why did Lindo's family leave her with the Huangs years before the wedding? (A flood destroyed their land.) Who seemed most unhappy about the separation? (her mother)
4. How was Lindo treated by the Huangs? (harshly) Did she submit to them? (She did as told.) Do you think her family knew how she would be treated?
5. Why was Lindo unhappy even before her wedding? (She was treated like a servant.) What sort of little boy was her future husband? (spoiled, self-centered) What sort of husband was he? (immature, unloving) Why didn't she run away? (She had nowhere to go.)
6. What sort of bad luck fell on Lindo's wedding day and night? (Japanese were near; there was a thunderstorm.) Do you think Lindo would have been happier if the wedding had been better-attended? (It mattered little to her.)
7. How did Lindo and her husband get along? (eventually, like sister and brother) Why did her mother-in-law treat her so harshly? (She wanted a grandson.) Do you think everyone—including Lindo—would have been happier if she had borne a son?

8.   What was Lindo's plan for getting out of her marriage? (She made up a dream that the ancestors were against the marriage and that a pregnant servant was bearing a royal son.) What does the plan show about the way her mind worked? (She understood her in-laws' snobbishness.) What else might she have tried?

9.   Why does Lindo buy gold bracelets? (to remind herself of her own worth, her ability to think for herself) Why does she mention her daughter's gold in the beginning of the story? (She thinks Waverly's gold means nothing.)

10.   What does Lindo do every year on the Festival of Pure Brightness? (removes her bracelets) Why? (to commemorate the day she found her own thoughts) If you were asked to name a day when you "knew a genuine thought and followed where it went" what day would you say that was?

Prediction: What sort of marriage will Lindo end up in the second time around?

Writing Idea: Imagine that you are Lindo's daughter, listening to the story of how she entered into her arranged marriage and then got out of it. Write the thoughts and questions that pass through your mind as you listen to her.

Ying-ying St. Clair: The Moon Lady—pages 64-88
The fourth story is told by the fourth mother, Ying-ying St. Clair. She recalls the day in 1918 when she was a little girl, lost by the lake at the Moon Festival. She watched a performance by the Moon Lady and ran onto the stage to have her wish granted. She was horrified to discover that the lovely Moon Lady was actually a man; only recently has Ying-ying been able to remember what her wish was: to be found.

Vocabulary
acrid 65	pungent 65	amah 65	tassel 67
rickshaw 71	presumptuous 72	pavilion 73	gingko 73
canopy 74	askew 74	warily 74	brigands 78
penance 80	wantonness 81		

Discussion Questions
1.   In this story and the last, we have seen that both Ying-ying and Lindo have some complaints about their daughters. How do their complaints compare? (They feel their daughters are thoughtless.)

2.   Who was Amah? (family servant who raised Ying-ying) How did she and Ying-ying get along? (They were like mother and daughter; Amah loved the girl, who took her for granted.) Was Ying-ying closer to her than to her own mother? (yes)

3. How did Amah define "ceremony"? (as the proper way to behave) Amah told Ying-ying to behave properly at the ceremony, not to shame Amah (p. 66). Where else in the book have you seen adults teaching children not to bring shame on others? (Lindo's and An-mei's stories) Do most parents today teach this?

4. How did Amah teach Ying-ying that it is wrong to think of her own needs? ("A girl can never ask, only listen."—p. 68) Where do you hear Ying-ying's mother making a similar point? (Girls stand still, don't chase dragonflies.) Is that what girls in the U.S. were being taught, at about the same time? (no)

5. What happened when Ying-ying discovered her shadow? (She had fun chasing it.) Do you have any similar memories? What do you think she means, "I loved my shadow, this dark side of me that had my same restless nature"?

6. Ying-ying says now that she was spoiled as a child because Amah never taught her to think about Amah's feelings. Do you think children should be taught to think about adults' feelings? How—or why not?

7. Did Ying-ying feel sorry for the rickshaw pullers—"panting like horses" (p. 72)? (no) In this story, what evidence do you find of the class system in China? (The fishermen realize Ying-ying is no beggar; she has been taught to ignore people like them.)

8. What are some of Ying-ying's most vivid memories of the boat ride? (the bird, falling into the water, seeing the Moon Lady) Are there any especially vivid early childhood memories you have of family outings?

9. How did Ying-ying get covered with blood? (She watched fish being cleaned.) Why was Amah so frightened? (She thought Ying-ying had been hurt.)

10. How does the Moon Lady story portray the roles of men and women? (Men are light and truth, women darkness and evil.) Why did little Ying-ying understand the Moon Lady's grief (p. 82)? (She was lost, afraid.) What frightened her when she drew close to the Moon Lady to tell her wish? Why do you think Ying-ying is finally able to remember that night—and the wish she made—now that she is old?

Prediction: What sort of woman does little Ying-ying grow up to be?

Supplementary Activities

Writing Idea: Ying-ying's earliest recollection is telling the Moon Lady her secret wish. Describe one of your earliest memories.

Literary Analysis: Theme
Explain that a **theme** is one of the central ideas of a literary work. Theme often concerns one of "life's truths." Titles, statements by characters, what characters learn, repeated phrases and images are often clues to the theme. The passing down of ritual

actions from mother to daughter is a theme developed throughout the first section. To elicit recognition of this theme from students, **ask:** Why is this section called "Feathers from a Thousand *Li* Away?" How does the italicized page relate to the four stories that follow? Why do the women want June to go to China? What did An-mei learn by watching her mother try to heal Popo? Why did Lindo agree to an arranged marriage she did not want? What did Ying-ying learn from the Moon Lady? What ceremonies and rituals are described in these stories? How are images of loss repeated through all four stories?

The Twenty-Six Malignant Gates

All four of these stories are about the mothers' attempts to protect their children.

Waverly Jong: Rules of the Game—pages 89-103

This story is told by Lindo's daughter, Waverly, who relates how she became a chess prodigy. The family lived in a meager flat above a Chinese bakery. When Waverly's brother received a used chess set at a Christmas party, Waverly read up on the rules at the library and began to play with a group of old men. Her mother began entering her in tournaments, and she collected trophy after trophy, to her mother's glee. Featured in *Life Magazine* as a child prodigy, Waverly nevertheless grew increasingly dissatisfied and unhappy. One day she blew up at her mother, saying she no longer wanted her mother to use her to show off.

Vocabulary

dim sum 90	prawns 91	benefactor 94	tactics 95
adversaries 95	benevolently 97	retort 97	etiquette 97
humility 97	prodigy 99	phlegmy 99	malodorous 100
concessions 101	careened 102		

Discussion Questions

1. What was the "art of invisible strength" that Waverly learned from her mother (p. 89)? (to bite your tongue when you want something) Do you think this is a good skill to have? Do you practice it?

2. Waverly says she didn't think her family was poor. Why not? (There was always enough food.) Were they? (They lived modestly.)

3. Why do you think Waverly shouted at the man who took the picture? What do you think her mother would have said, if she had seen what happened?

4. How did Waverly get her name? (from the street the family lived on) What did her family call her? (Mei-mei—little sister) Where else do you see the importance of names mentioned in these stories? (Tyan-yu, p. 44)

5. Who put on the annual Christmas party? (church missionary ladies) Where else have you seen "missionary ladies" mentioned in the story? (They gave June's parents gifts, p. 6.)

6. Why do you think Waverly's mother said the chess set was "too good," although it was obviously used—then told Winston to throw it out when they got home? (She wanted to be polite and respectful, but had some pride.)

7. Who taught Waverly the rules of chess? (her brothers, library books, men on the street) What do you think her mother meant when she said it was important for foreign people to find out the rules themselves (p. 95)?

8. How did Waverly's family encourage her to play chess? (They took her to tournaments, gave her her own room, let her leave her food unfinished.) Do you think they would have encouraged her to excel at sports? art? science?

9. How did Waverly feel about being a chess prodigy? (proud, but angry that her mother showed her off, took credit) Would you like to have been a famous prodigy? If so, what sort? What would be some drawbacks?

10. How was going to the shops with her mother a "duty" for Waverly? (Her mother insisted on taking her and bragging to everyone.) What caused the argument she had on the street? (Waverly told her to stop showing her off.) Have you ever been in a situation like this? How could Waverly and her mother have handled the situation better?

    Prediction: What will be Waverly's "next move" after the argument with her mother?

Writing Idea: Waverly tells how she got her official name and her nickname. Tell how you got your name(s).

Lena St. Clair: The Voice from the Wall—pages 104-121

Ying-ying's daughter, Lena, remembers the family's moving from their apartment in Oakland to another in San Francisco. Her mother saw danger in everything. The mother's fears grew worse during pregnancy, and when her pregnancy culminated tragically in a stillbirth, she had a nervous breakdown. Lena heard the neighbors arguing loudly, she imagined the worst; however, when she met the Sorci girl, she realized that the family was basically a loving one.

Vocabulary

    chasm 105   Caucasian 106

Discussion Questions

1. How did Lena imagine the death of the beggar? (His mind was broken.) Would you call her an imaginative child? How is the idea of being "pulled through the wall" used both in the beginning and the end of this story? (The beggar pulls the great-grandfather; Lena pulls her mother.)

2. How did Lena's mother try to keep her out of the basement? (with frightening stories about a man down there) Why? (so she wouldn't get hurt) What was the result? (Lena was terrified of the basement and many other things.) Do you think it is ever a good idea to play on a child's fears in order to protect him?

3. What sort of terrible things did Lena see? (playground equipment killing children, a devil in the sandbox) Were these imaginings? hallucinations? Why does she say she saw them with her "Chinese eyes" (p. 106)? (They are like her mother's fearful eyes, seeing danger everywhere.)

4. Why did Lena's father think he had "saved" her mother? (He had married her and taken her to America—p. 107.) Do you think he also contributed to her sense of being lost?

5. Why do you think Lena's mother was so worried about her walking straight home from school? What did she say might happen to Lena? Do you think anything like this ever happened to the mother?

6. How did the family "move up"—both literally and figuratively? (They moved to a better apartment—from Oakland to the hills of San Francisco.) Why didn't Lena's mother like the hills and the apartment's walls and doors? (She saw strength and good fortune running away down the hill.) How did the red-faced man throw her "off balance"? (He yelled and lurched toward her and Lena.)

7. How did Lena's mother act when she was pregnant? (agitated) Do you agree with her father that her behavior was due to "nesting instincts"? Do you think he should have tried to get help for her? What would you do if someone in your family started acting depressed or agitated, as she did?

8. Why was Lena worried about the unborn baby? (Her mother bumped into things.) How did these fears turn out to be justified? (The baby was stillborn.) Have you ever had irrational fears that were later realized in actuality?

9. Trace references to the "worst possible thing that could happen" in this story. Do you think it is better to imagine the worst, so that you can avoid it—or to put such thoughts out of your mind?

10. How was Lena affected by her encounter with the neighbors? (She learned the world isn't always a dangerous place; her neighbors fight but love each other.) Why did she want to "save" her own mother? (She saw that her mother's fears were unjustified.) Was she successful in her dream? (Yes—she pulled her mother through the wall, back to reality.)

Prediction: What will the "tragedy she could not speak about" in Ying-ying's past turn out to be?

Writing Idea: Describe what Teresa saw when she walked into Lena's room.

Research: Find out more about the history of Angel Island. What were the detention camps like?

Rose Hsu Jordan: Half and Half—pages 122-140

An-mei's daughter, Rose, reveals that she and her husband Ted, a dermatologist, are about to divorce. Ted's mother had never approved of her son's marrying an Asian-American woman. Rose reflects on how her loss of faith in her husband is similar to her mother's loss of faith after the tragic death of Rose's younger brother. The parents had taken their seven children to the beach and Rose had been assigned to watch four-year-old Bing, who disappeared into the surf. An-mei could not accept his death.

Vocabulary

chagrined 123	brashness 123	dermatology 125	regal 135

Discussion Questions

1. Why did Rose's mother put the bible under the table? (She lost faith after her son drowned.) Where have you seen references to "correcting imbalances" in earlier stories? (in the previous story; in Lindo's story, p. 59)
2. What sort of person is Ted? (arrogant, cold) Why do you think Rose and Ted were initially attracted to each other? Why did they grow apart?
3. How did Rose's and Ted's family feel about the relationship? (Both families disapproved.) Do you think the marriage would have lasted if the families had been more supportive?
4. In what ways were Ted and Rose always "saving and being saved"? (Rose played the victim, Ted the hero.) Where have you seen this theme before? (Lena's father thought he had saved Ying-ying; Lena wanted to save her mother.)
5. How did the malpractice suit change Ted? (He wanted Rose to make more of the decisions.) Why do you suppose he began pushing Rose to make decisions? Do you see as a strength or a weakness Rose's tendency to spend a lot of time weighing pros and cons? Do you prefer to be the one who makes decisions or the one who goes along with someone else's decision? What is the Taoist view of decision-making? (One should just let things happen.)

6. Why did Rose's mother lose her faith? (Her son died.) Do you agree with Rose that maybe "faith was just an illusion that somehow you're in control" (p. 128)?

7. What is *nengkan*—p. 128? (ability to do anything you try) Do you believe in your ability to do anything you put your mind to? Do you think Rose's father still believed in his *nengkan* after that day at the beach?

8. Rose has a vivid memory of Bing as she last saw him—"I still see him, so clearly that I almost feel I can make him stay there forever" (p. 132). Have you ever felt that way? Have you ever wished you could stop time at a particular moment to keep someone safe?

9. Which family members do you think felt guilty about Bing's death? (Everyone blamed themselves.) Do you think Rose should feel guilty? Do you think An-mei expected to succeed in "bringing back" Bing? How do you think family life changed after Bing's death?

10. Do you agree with Rose that she just "let it happen" when it came to both Bing's death and the breakup of her marriage? Her mother tells her that she should try to save her marriage whether there is any hope or not. Do you agree? Has her mother taught her by example to do what she exhorts—"think for yourself" (p. 140)? (She tried to change Bing's fate.)

Prediction: Will Rose try to save her marriage?

Writing Idea: Describe a time when you did not act because you found making a choice too difficult. Describe the consequences and explain whether you are glad or not that you let the choice be taken out of your hands.

Jing-mei Woo: Two Kinds—pages 141-160

Jing-mei recounts her late mother's unsuccessful attempts to turn her into a child prodigy. With each trial—the Shirley Temple hairdo, the memory tests—Jing-mei grew more resistant. When her mother arranged piano lessons with deaf Mr. Chong, Jing-mei practiced lazily, without correcting herself. On the day of the big talent show, she played terribly—the first of many disappointments her mother felt in her. It wasn't until years later, after her mother's death, that she realized that the piece she had played so poorly—"Pleading Child"—had a companion piece, "Perfectly Contented."

Vocabulary

reproach 143	bellows 144	mesmerizing 145	arpeggios 148
staccato 148	preludes 148	discordant 148	debut 149
sulky 150	fiasco 152	nonchalantly 152	reconditioned 155

Discussion Questions

1. Jing-mei's mother believed that in America you could be anything you wanted to be. Do you agree? Where have you seen this attitude before in the book? (All the parents feel this way.) Where in this story do you again see ideas that have been raised in previous stories about balance—"yin and yang"? (the titles of the two piano pieces; Jing-mei's confidence and excitement, then failure)

2. How do you explain that Jing-mei's mother lost everything in China, yet never looked back with regret? Have you ever known anyone like that? Do you think other members of the Joy Luck Club are like that?

3. Jing-mei's mother, like Waverly's, liked the idea of a prodigy. Was the same motivation involved with both mothers? (Waverly learned chess on her own; June was pushed to succeed.) Why do you suppose one mother produced a prodigy—and the other didn't? (Waverly was "a natural;" June wasn't.)

4. Why did Jing-mei like the idea of being a prodigy at first—but not later? (She realized that she wasn't cut out to be one.) What is ironic about the picture of a mother trying to train her child to be a prodigy? (One either is or isn't a prodigy.)

5. Why did Jing-mei resist becoming a good piano player? (She didn't want someone else defining her.) Do you think she could have been good? Have you ever resisted something your parents wanted for you?

6. Jing-mei thought, "I won't be what I'm not" (p. 144). Have you seen other characters in the book with this attitude? (Lindo escaped her arranged marriage.) Of the four daughters, which one do you think is most "true to herself"? Why do you suppose that is?

7. What did Jing-mei's mother sacrifice for her to have piano lessons? (Her mother did housekeeping for Mr. Chong.) Did Jing-mei appreciate the sacrifice? (no) Why? (because she didn't care about the lessons) Have you ever appreciated a sacrifice your parents made for you—but not until much later?

8. Why was the talent show such a disaster? (Jing-mei didn't practice hard, played terribly.) Have you ever experienced anything like this? Do you think Jing-mei's parents handled the aftermath well? What would you say to your child after such a performance?

9. How does the blow-up Jing-mei had with her mother compare with the one Waverly had with her mother? (Both daughters were fed up with trying to please their mothers.) Why did Jing-mei bring up the babies? (She knew it would put an end to the argument; she'd have the last word.) Have you ever exploded like that? Why did both daughters meet with the silent treatment? (They had been disrespectful, so were "shunned.")

Prediction: Will Jing-mei always feel that she has failed her mother?

Supplementary Activities

Writing Idea: When Jing-mei's mother offered her the piano, she saw the offer as a "sign of forgiveness, a tremendous burden removed." Write a short story—real or imagined—about a gift you received that was a welcome sign of forgiveness.

Literary Analysis: Figurative Language
Explain the distinction between **metaphor** and **simile**. (A simile is an expressed analogy; a metaphor an implied one.) Point out several examples in the first section. (e.g., "She died just like a rabbit"—p. 5; "…we would come back out like newborn kittens"—p. 9; "…my mother's life has been shelved for new business"—p. 17). Ask students to identify what two things are being compared, and how that comparison makes the detail more vivid. Ask students to cite other examples of figurative language.

American Translation
All four of these stories are about how the daughters have or have not synthesized the traditions of their mothers.

Lena St. Clair: Rice Husband—pages 161-181
Lena's mother is about to visit Lena and her husband, Harold, and Lena wonders what Ying-ying will see of the tensions in her marriage. She and Harold met at the architectural firm where they both work. Although he is a partner and she is an associate, they have always split expenses down the middle. In fact, he often allowed her to pay more than her share when they were dating and appropriated many of her ideas during his rise within the company. Lena's mother is not happy about what she finds on her arrival—the list of shared expenses, including ice cream she knows Lena never eats, the unstable table Harold insists on keeping in the guest room. As Lena and Harold argue downstairs, they hear the crash of glass as the table in Ying-ying's room falls.

Vocabulary
embezzlement 161	remorse 165	pustules 166	anorexic 166
sham 169	Tao 170	ethnicity 170	karma 170
intuitive 170	domestic 174	trellis 174	bougainvillea 174
prenuptial 175	philosophical 176	minimalist 178	lacquer 178
manipulative 179			

Discussion Questions

1. What is the connection between the italicized page (159) and the story that follows? (Both are about Ying-ying's visit to Lena's.) What does the mother see in the mirror? (her grandson) Do you think the daughter puts up the mirror where her mother suggests?

2. What do you learn about Lena's father that you did not know before? (He has died.) Which part of this story have you heard before? (the stillborn child)

3. What problems are Lena and Harold having? (Lena is irritated with Harold's ways of splitting costs, always being "fair.") Do you think there is genuine affection between these two?

4. How is Lena and Harold's marriage like the table that Harold made? (both are unstable) Is their relationship worth trying to save? Do you think it will last?

5. Why does Lena feel that she has to pretend nothing is the matter while her mother is there? (She has always tried to act in ways that won't upset her emotionally volatile mother.) Does she succeed? (No—her mother knows.)

6. When Lena was eight, why did her mother tell her she would marry a bad man? (to get her to finish her rice) Why is Lena thinking about that, now? (She is in a faltering marriage.) Why is the memory nauseating to her, rather than funny? (She is very upset with her current life—as if the rice story has come true.)

7. There are several references to missionary ladies and the church in this book. What role does the Sunday school teacher play in this story? (She shows a film about lepers.)

8. Why did Lena think that by not eating, she would not have to marry Arnold? (He would get more pockmarked, die of leprosy.) Would you say that this was the start of a lifelong eating disorder? Why did Lena blame herself for Arnold's death? (She had hoped for it, and quit eating.) Why did she gorge herself on ice cream that night? (Maybe she thought eating would bring him back.)

9. Lena thinks about her hatred of Arnold and says, "Isn't hate merely the result of wounded love?" Do you think it is? Do you think her anger at her husband is also the result of wounded love?

10. How has Lena helped Harold's career? (She gave him ideas for theme restaurants.) Do you think he shows her that he values her creativity? Does she show him that she values him? Do you think she is right in feeling that he is fair to everyone but her? How does he respond when she asserts herself? (He acts patronizing.) Do you think any of the fault for the inequity lies with her? Do any of her complaints sound petty to you?

Prediction: Will Harold and Lena be happier together in the future?

Writing Idea: Suppose a marriage counselor has asked Lena and Harold to make two lists—what each values about the other and what changes each would like to see in the marriage. Compose Lena's lists.

Waverly Jong: Four Directions—pages 182-205

Waverly, divorced now, with a four-year-old daughter, is nervous about meeting her hypercritical mother at the Four Directions restaurant. She has planned to tell Lindo that she is going to marry her current boyfriend, Rich, but puts it off. The reader learns that after ten-year-old Waverly had the shouting match with her mother following the chess match, she quit playing for a while. When she resumed, her mother was much less involved in the games and Waverly found that she had lost her confidence. She quit playing for good at fourteen, married Marvin Chen at eighteen, had a child, separated and later met Rich, a kind and loving man. When Waverly finally finds the courage to tell her mother that she and Rich are getting married, she is surprised and relieved by her mother's response ("I already know this") and even half-considers inviting her mother to join them on their honeymoon trip to China.

Vocabulary

pristine 185	sonorous 192	contempt 192	apathetic 192
puritanical 193	translucent 193	inviolable 193	innuendos 193
sullied 194	amorous 198	guileless 199	acquiesced 200
quavering 201	soothed 202	stalemate 203	uncanny 204

Discussion Questions

1. Why has Waverly taken her mother to lunch? (to soften her up for the news that Waverly is marrying Rich) Have you ever tried to "butter up" your mother before dropping certain news on her? Did it work better than it worked for Waverly?

2. Why didn't Waverly's mother want to give the waiter a tip? (She felt the soup was cold, chop sticks greasy, etc.) Why do you think mother and daughter have such different attitudes toward money?

3. Do you think this mother and daughter understand each other pretty well? Where do you find Waverly still using chess terms to describe her interactions with her mother? (pages 191,199) Why do you suppose that is?

4. How can you tell that Waverly still seeks her mother's approval? (She is afraid to announce her marriage plans.) Why do you suppose that approval is so important to her? Does her mother usually withhold approval? (She is hypercritical of things.)

5. Waverly's mother paid a lot of attention to her when she had the chicken pox. Why did this make Waverly so happy? (Waverly figured things were finally back to normal after the blow-up on the street.) Do you think she had been afraid she

had lost her mother's love? Or was she feeling more gratified that she had "beaten" her mother?

6. How do you explain the change in Waverly's mother's attitude toward her chess playing? Why did Waverly feel that her mother was "erecting an invisible wall" (p. 190)? Hadn't she wanted her mother to be less involved in her chess playing? Do you think her mother was trying to respect her wishes? trying to punish her? trying to get her to make her own choices?

7. Why was Waverly so afraid of telling her mother she was going to marry Rich? (She was afraid her mother's criticism would sway her own opinion of Rich.) Do you think she was right in anticipating that her mother would attack him? If Waverly loves Rich, why would she care so much about any criticisms her mother has, anyway?

8. Why do you suppose Waverly eloped at such a young age? Why do you think that bothered her mother so much? What had her mother's experience with early marriage been? (She had been miserable.) Did it work out for Waverly? (no) Was she right in thinking her mother might have "poisoned" her marriage?

9. How is Rich's love for Waverly "unequivocal" (p.193)? (He loves her just for herself.) What do most people want in a relationship? Is Rich the sort of person you would picture her marrying, given the impression you have formed of her from the rest of the book?

10. What does Waverly mean, "I couldn't save Rich in the kitchen. And I couldn't save him later at the dinner table" (p.196)? (She thinks he made a bad impression on her mother.) Did her mother disapprove of him? (Waverly thought so.)

11. Why does Waverly's mother start talking about Genghis Khan and Sun Yat-sen? (She is trying to show her daughter that she loves her, understands her confusion about her dual nature.) How does her explanation of what is inside Waverly hark back to the theme of "yin and yang"? (Waverly is of "two kinds" according to her mother.) Does Waverly understand what she is saying? (yes) Do you think mother and daughter understand each other better after this conversation?

Prediction: Will Lindo accompany Waverly and Rich to China?

Writing Idea: Reread Waverly's description of her mother on page 204: "I could finally see what was really there: an old woman, a wok for her armor, a knitting needle for her sword, getting a little crabby as she waited patiently for her daughter to invite her in."

Using a similar structure, describe what you see when you look at someone you know well:__________, a____ for her ______, a _______ for her _________, getting a little ______ as she ___________________________________.

Rose Hsu Jordan: Without Wood—pages 206-220

Rose tells of meeting her mother at a funeral and mentioning that Ted had sent her a $10,000 check. Her mother speculated—rightly, it turned out—that he was "doing monkey business" with another woman. Her mother had once told her that she was "without wood" and therefore listened to too many people. This time she decides not to go along meekly with her husband's request that she sign the divorce papers and give up the house.

Vocabulary

cremated 209	inventoried 212	sentimental 214	foyer 214
obsessively 214	flagstone 215	despicable 217	refuge 218

Discussion Questions

1. How did the words Rose's mother spoke come from up high—literally and figuratively? (Rose was looking up from bed at her mother, who assured Rose she knew her "inside out.") When you were little, did you—like Rose—believe everything your mother said? Did your mother—like Rose's—continually stress the importance of listening to her?

2. Why would Rose's mother ask her if she were ready to see Mr. Chou? (to prepare her for sleep) Did anyone ever tell you about something similar—like the Sandman—when you were going to sleep? How did the Mr. Chou story backfire? (Rose was afraid he would bring her bad dreams.)

3. Why do you suppose Amy Tan has Rose and her mother hold their conversation about the divorce at a funeral ceremony? Do you find anything humorous about this? What does the mother's opinion of psychiatrists seem to be? (negative) Has Rose's experience been otherwise? (Hers seems bored, uninterested.)

4. Why is Rose "seeing *heimongmong*"? (She is angry about the way Ted is treating her, feels overwhelmed, confused.) Have you ever felt that way?

5. Why do you think Rose has told each person something different about how she is feeling about Ted? Have you ever done that? Can each version be true?

6. How did Rose's mother figure out that Rose's husband was having an affair with someone else? (Rose mentioned that she got a check from Ted, which her mother finds suspiciously uncharacteristic.) Why do you suppose Rose was the "last to know"?

7. What was Rose's mother saying when she once told her she was "without wood"? (She is indecisive, listens too much to others.) Where do you see the mother's prediction that she will "grow wild...until someone pulls you out and throws you away" (p. 213) echoed later in the story? (At the end, Rose decides she likes the overgrown garden—and decides to fight Ted.)

8. What do you think of Ted? Do you have any sympathy for him? Do you think he is as despicable as Rose decides he is? Why do you think he enclosed the check?

9. Why does Rose decide not to sign the papers? (She wants the house, decides not to passively go along with Ted's plan.) Do you think she is making the right decision? Why does she show him the garden? (She knows it will irritate him.) Why does she enjoy scaring him? (He has scared her for years.)

10. What do you make of the dream that Rose has? Is it basically a good dream or a nightmare?

Prediction: How will Ted and Rose's divorce turn out?

Writing Idea: You are Rose. Write the notes you will take with you to the lawyer, in which you list what you want.

Jing-mei Woo: Best Quality—pages 221-240

June recalls the day five months ago when her mother gave her a jade pendant after a crab dinner. First, June had tried to take the crab with the missing leg from the serving plate. Later, Waverly informed her that the reason she hadn't been paid for a piece of advertising copy she had done was that her superiors had decided it was not good enough. In the kitchen after dinner, June's mother pointed out that the crab with the missing leg had been bad—and that June, unlike Waverly and the others, is true to her own nature, rather than always demanding "best quality." With that, she removed the necklace from her own neck and gave it to June.

Vocabulary

garishly 221	oblong 222	ruse 223	snickered 229
humiliated 232	carcasses 232	tofu 236	

Discussion Questions

1. Why did June start to take the legless crab? (She didn't particularly like crab.) Why did June's mother use the chipped dishes? (She forgot the nice ones she had been saving.) Do you think the mother and daughter are alike?

2. June's mother gave her a pendant—and Lindo's mother gave Lindo one. Were these gestures similar? (Both were signs of the mother's trust in her daughter, desire to pass on something of herself.)

3. How did Waverly manage to insult June while complimenting her haircut? (She suggested June didn't pay much for it.) When did you see Waverly on the receiving end of an insult about her own haircut? (at the restaurant with her mother)

4. June mentions that Waverly learned from her mother the skill of choosing the best. How did Waverly pick one of the best Christmas presents, as a child? (She realized small, heavy packages may be better than big ones, and so chose the Lifesavers.) When Lindo was young, was she always in a position to choose the best? (No, her family was not well-off.)

5. Why was June upset after dinner? (Waverly had cut her—and her writing ability—down.) Does this sort of thing often happen at family dinners? Who—if anyone—do you feel was out of line?

6. Did June's mother try to comfort her in the kitchen? (Yes, she told her daughter she was unique—true to herself.) Do you think she said the "right thing" to her daughter?

7. Do you think that June's mother's assessment of the difference between Waverly and June is correct? (She implies that June is more honest and direct.) Is she saying that June is more genuine, less pretentious? Why had she said before that June was not sophisticated, like Waverly? (She was probably being sarcastic about Waverly.) Do you think June understood? (She felt betrayed.)

8. Why is June making a spicy bean curd dish? (It was one her mother used to make for her father.) What is the connection between this scene and the previous one, where her mother gave her the pendant? How is she "filling in," again, for her dead mother? (She cooks for her father, tries to chase away the cat.)

9. Did June think her mother killed the cat? (She wasn't sure.) Did you?
   Prediction: After June's mother dies, what will June wish she had asked her?

Supplementary Activities

Writing Idea: Write a conversation that you have with your mother in the kitchen. Make the dialogue sound as realistic as possible.

Literary Analysis: Naturalistic Dialogue

Point out that many critics have praised Amy Tan for having a "fine ear for dialogue." Have them examine specific examples of dialogue in this section to see what makes the conversations sound so realistic. For example, she reproduces several mothers' exclamations and broken English (p. 162—Ying-ying; p. 182—Lindo; p. 209—An-mei; and p. 224—Suyuan). She injects humor by showing how the mothers sometimes misinterpret what they hear (e.g., p. 224—"I not from Fukien. Hunh! He know nothing!") And she does an equally masterful job of reproducing the daughters' more sophisticated, Americanized, "Valley Girl" dialect—(e.g., p. 231 "Listen, June...That stuff you wrote, well, the firm decided it was unacceptable").

Queen Mother of the Western Skies

The last four stories are about the sacrifices the mothers have made for their daughters.

An-mei Hsu: Magpies—pages 240-273

Told that her daughter is divorcing, An-mei thinks back to a story her mother (the concubine) once told her. When the mother was a girl, Popo had forbidden her to cry. That night she cried by the pond and a turtle ate her tears. From its beak poured out seven eggs and from these hatched seven magpies, birds of joy. She learned from that to swallow her tears, lest they feed someone else's joy. Later, as a lovely young widow, she was tricked into becoming a concubine for a wealthy merchant, Wu-Tsing, so that she could bear him a son. Her family disowned her and raised her two children, but she eventually retrieved An-mei and took her to live in the rich merchant's household. She secured An-mei's future by killing herself, so that the repentant old man would raise the little girl well. An-mei wants her daughter to know that women no longer have to swallow their tears.

Vocabulary

quince 247	porter 249	laments 250	canopy 252
commotion 258	reckless 260	docile 263	lute 264
pagoda 266	conspired 266		

Discussion Questions

1. In the italicized story on p. 239, what does the grandmother call the baby? (Queen Mother) Where have we seen the Queen Mother of the Western Skies before? (p. 81)
2. Why did the family treat An-mei's mother so coldly? (She had become a concubine.) Why do you think she didn't speak back to them?
3. How did An-mei's mother become a concubine? (She was tricked into it.) Where do you learn this? (Yan Chang, her mother's personal maid, told An-mei.)
4. Why did Wu-Tsing's wife pick An-mei's mother? (She was lovely, would produce a fine son.) Why was it so important for Wu-Tsing to have a son? (tradition)
5. What sort of mother do you suppose Popo was? Why did An-mei's mother allow her to raise her own daughter? (She was not given a choice, was sent away after she "disgraced" the family. She probably felt ashamed as well.) Do you think she worried about the way Popo would raise An-mei?
6. Why do you think An-mei's mother came back when Popo was ill? (She really was a good daughter, but was the victim of Wu-Tsing and society.) Did she love Popo? (She respected her, which may have been more important than love.)

7. How did Wu-Tsing's second wife gain power over people? (She fed Wife #1's opium addiction, gave presents, staged "pretend suicides.") Why did she give An-mei the necklace? (to win her favor) Why did her mother crush it? (to show An-mei it was as false as Wife #2)

8. Why did An-mei's mother kill herself? (so that the merchant would take pity on her daughter and raise her comfortably) Do you think An-mei ever felt as if her mother's death were her own fault?

9. How does An-mei want things to be different for her daughter than they were for her? (She wants her to be a strong, independent woman and to be able to make her own choices.)

    Prediction: Will An-mei's daughter learn how to lose her innocence—but not her hope?

Writing Idea: Describe the memory An-mei's mother has as she hurries back to her dying mother's bedside.

Ying-ying St. Clair: Waiting Between the Trees—pages 274-287

Lena and her husband Harold have invited Lena's mother to stay at their place while her building is being rewired. Ying-ying sees signs of imbalance in the marriage—most notably, a list of shared expenses Harold carefully keeps and a table he has made which—like the marriage—may look elegant, but is unstable. She recalls what she never told Lena about her past—the philandering husband who left her, the child she aborted, the kind American she married without loving. Born in the year of the Tiger, she waits "between the trees" and knows what will happen: the table will break and she will cut loose her daughter's tiger spirit by telling her about her mother's past.

Vocabulary

    smirk 275   cobblestone 276

Discussion Questions

1. How does this story pick up where another one left off? (See "Rice Husband,"-p. 161.) Is the mother's version of things the same as the daughter's version? (no)

2. Why does Ying-ying feel that her daughter needs to be "saved"? (Lena has no spirit.) How does she plan to do it? (by revealing her own unhappy past)

3. Do you think Lena was being disrespectful when she laughed at her mother's mispronunciation (p. 275)? Have you seen the daughters pointing out the mothers' deficiencies in English throughout the story? (yes) Are the daughters embarrassed by their mothers? (sometimes)

4. Why does Ying-ying remember "Uncle" (p. 277) so vividly? Are the memories pleasant? (He married her, then abandoned her.)

5. Why was it an evil thing when "Uncle" cut open the watermelon? (He was being lascivious.)

6. Why did Ying-ying marry this older man? (She saw a sign that she should; her family supported the marriage.) Are you surprised that her family supported the marriage? Do you think they knew his reputation for womanizing? Did they care about Ying-ying's happiness?

7. How did Ying-ying learn about her husband's philandering? (Her youngest aunt told her.) What was her reaction? (She was angry, broken-hearted.) What happened to her baby? (She aborted it.) Do you think she felt guilty later? How did she react, later, when her other baby was stillborn? (sank into depression)

8. In what ways is Ying-ying a Tiger? (She was born under that sign; sees what others cannot.)

9. How did Ying-ying's life change after her husband's betrayal? (She felt helpless, humiliated and ashamed, lived in poor conditions, worked as a shopgirl.) How long was it before she met Clifford St. Clair? (about ten years)

10. Why do you think St. Clair courted Ying-ying for so long? (He wanted to help her, save her.) Do you think she loved him? Do you think he ever regretted marrying her?

Prediction: What do you think Ying-ying says to Lena when Lena comes upstairs?

Writing Idea: Reread Ying-ying's description of her feelings for St. Clair on p. 284: "I neither liked him nor disliked him. I thought him neither attractive nor unattractive..." Use this sentence pattern as the model for a description of your own. "I thought (him) (her) neither...nor..."

Lindo Jong: Double Face—pages 288-305

As Lindo gets her hair done for Waverly's second wedding (Waverly wants her mother to look more chic), Lindo thinks about her "two faces"—Chinese and American. She always wanted her children to have the best of both worlds, but Waverly isn't Chinese—even though she sometimes wants to be, now that it is fashionable. She tells Waverly about the hardships she met on arrival in this country. She met An-mei while working in a fortune cookie factory and through An-mei, she met her future husband. They went to English class together, married, had a son, Winston, (who died at 16 in a car accident), another son, Vincent, then Waverly. Lindo notices that Waverly has her crooked nose, and Lindo thinks again about her two faces—Chinese and American.

Vocabulary

    longevity 293   spouse 302

Discussion Questions

1. Why was Lindo at Rory's? (Waverly convinced her to get her hair done there for Waverly's wedding.) She feels that her daughter is criticizing her hair. When did we see her criticize Waverly's haircut, in another story? (She had told Waverly her asymmetrical cut was crooked.)
2. Why do you think Waverly has chosen China for her second honeymoon?
3. Would you say that Waverly has rejected her Chinese heritage? Why is she suddenly so interested in it? (Being Chinese has become fashionable.)
4. Why do you think it displeases Waverly when Rory says that she looks like her mother? Would a comment like that please or displease you?
5. Do you think Lindo's mother criticized her much when she was a girl? Do you think her predictions about her daughter's appearance and future as a "good wife, mother, and daughter-in-law" turned out to be true?
6. Why did Waverly's mother try to hide her Chinese face as soon as she came to this country (p. 294)? (She thought it was necessary in order to get ahead.) Isn't that the very thing she is critical of Waverly for doing now? (yes)
7. What was Lindo's first job in this country? (She worked in a fortune cookie factory.) How did she like it? (She burned her fingers and worked hard, but made a good friend.) How did it lead to her meeting her husband? (An-mei introduced her to her future husband.) How does the theme of "fortune telling" thread throughout this story? (Lindo's mother saw fortunes in faces.)
8. What happened to Waverly's oldest brother? (He died in a car crash.) In what scene did he appear once in an earlier story? (He chose the model submarine as his toy.) Are you surprised that his death is not treated in more detail?
9. In what tone do you imagine Lindo asking Waverly, "Why do you always tell your friends that I arrived in the United States on a slow boat from China" (p. 295)? Do you think Waverly is being disrespectful? Is she embarrassed by her mother? Is her mother hurt?
10. Does Lindo regret that she has become so "Americanized"? (somewhat) She decides to ask Waverly what she thinks (p. 305). What do you think Waverly will say?

    Prediction: Will Waverly identify more strongly with her "Chinese" self at some point in the future?

Writing Idea: You are helping An-mei and Lindo look through the fortunes for the right instructions to give Lindo's future husband. List five fortunes that might work.

Jing-mei Woo: A Pair of Tickets—pages 306-332

June and her father have left Hong Kong by train for Shenzhen, China. They go to Guangzhou, where they are met by her father's aunt and relatives. They all go to the elegant, modestly-priced hotel room where June and her father have reservations. That evening, they all eat hamburgers and apple pie. Late that night, June hears her father explain how his late wife tried for many years to locate the twins she left by the roadside as she ran away from the Japanese, sure that she herself was near death and that leaving the twins was their best chance for survival. Only years later—shortly after June's mother died—did a former schoolmate locate the twins, who had been raised by a loving old peasant couple. The couple had been unable to read the note asking the twins' finders to bring them to their father, but they had kept the pictures with the girls' names written on them, and because of this the connection was made years later. June and her father take a plane to Shanghai, where they have an emotional meeting with June's half-sisters—the fulfillment of her mother's long-cherished wish.

Vocabulary

transforming 308	declaration forms 312	Mongol 312	relic 315
unrestrained 316	scaffolding 317	bamboo 317	itinerary 318
sheepish 318	hoisin sauce 320	forlorn 320	surname 322
barter 324	missionary 326	dysentery 326	pious 327

Discussion Questions

1. On the train to China, June realizes she has "never really known what it means to be Chinese." Do you think she knows by the end of her trip? Have you ever had any desire to visit the place(s) of your ancestors?

2. What do you think June's father is thinking and feeling as he looks out the train window?

3. How and when were the twins discovered? (After June's mother died they wrote to her. One of Suyuan's classmates had recognized them and called them by name. They recognized their original names from the pictures she had put in their little shirts years ago.) Do you consider this a believable coincidence? Would the story be better if June's mother had learned of their survival before her death?

4. What is the reunion with June's father's aunt and other relatives like? (lots of hugs, tears) How do you think she feels as everyone talks around her? What does June learn about herself and her family from this reunion? (She hears the story of why her mother left the twins by the roadside and how her entire family was killed when the house in Shanghai was bombed.)

5. How did June's mother know that her entire family had been killed? (The house had been flattened; she found the doll she had given her niece.) Why do you suppose this wasn't one of the stories that June had heard many times?

6. Why does June keeping saying, "This is Communist China"? What evidence does she see of how China has changed? (The hotel is lavish; there is a lot of westernization.)

7. Why do you suppose June's mother didn't tell her father she was looking for the twins all these years? Was she ashamed of leaving them? (She must have known in her heart she did what she thought at the time was best for them.) What do you imagine went through her mind all those years? Does this story help explain why Suyuan had such high hopes for Jing-mei? (Perhaps she unconsciously wished Jing-mei could fill the void of the loss of the twins.)

8. Why is Aiyi surprised to hear that Suyuan fled the Japanese when they came to Kweilin? How was history "rewritten"? (It wasn't commonly reported that the Japanese had marched on Kweilin.)

9. When do you think June's father first learned why his wife had left the babies? Why do you suppose she never told him?

10. What do you see, hear, feel as you read the description of June's reunion with her two half-sisters? How is it that "together we look like our mother" (p. 332)? (Together, they are the China Suyuan left behind, and the America where she found a new life.)

Supplementary Activities

Writing Idea: You are June. Write two entries in your travel diary—one after your stay at the hotel and one after the reunion at the airport.

Literary Analysis: Narrative Point of View
Explain that the point of view is the vantage point from which the author tells the story—through whose eyes the story is told. There are two basic ways an author may present the events in the story: first person narrator ("I") or third person narrator ("he/she").
Ask: What is unusual about the point of view in this book?
The point of view switches in each story. This technique is known as "multiple points of view," and is used more frequently in contemporary literature than it was in the past. Each mother narrates two stories and each daughter (except June) narrates two stories. Jing-mei narrates all four stories about her family, since her mother is dead.

Postreading Questions
for Discussion or Writing

1. How are these sixteen stories related and arranged? What do the italicized stories that precede each section have to do with the sections that follow? What repeating patterns did you notice throughout the book? What is the significance of section and story titles?

2. What do the mothers in these stories want for their daughters? Which one(s) would you consider "good mothers"? What do the daughters want from their mothers? What do you think Amy Tan is saying about the mother-daughter relationship? about heritage? about memory?

3. What does the role of men seem to be in this story? What would you say to someone who states, "Amy Tan gives an unfair and incomplete portrayal of Asian and Asian-American men in her book"?

4. What did you learn from this book about Chinese history and culture? How much of the experience described in these stories is uniquely Chinese or Chinese-American? Which elements of these stories are universal? What did Amy Tan have to know in order to write this book?

5. What emotions did you experience while reading these stories? Where did you laugh? cry? feel surprised? shocked? sympathetic? What struck you as you read the book? What one quote from the book is most memorable to you?

6. To which character(s) could you "relate"? Which ones did you like? Which ones did you understand? Which ones did you want to protect? In which ones did you notice changes? Would you have reacted as they did? What would you like to say to them? What do you wish some of these characters had said to each other—but did not?

7. Did these stories and characters remind you of any others? Were you reminded of any particular songs, poems, paintings, movies? events in your own life?

8. Do you have any advice for any of these characters? Which ones do you think made good choices? Which could have made better choices?

9. What did you think of the ending to the book? Why do you suppose Amy Tan had Jing-mei Woo tell both the first and the last stories? How are the last story and the first one linked? Are there any questions still on your mind after you finish the last page?

10. Are these stories believable? How does Amy Tan bring these stories to life? How much do you think came from her own experience? What do you notice about her writing technique? What sort of readers would most enjoy this book?

Postreading Activities

Related Reading

The Asian-American Experience —Stories by three contemporary Asian American
   writers: Maxine Hong Kingston, David Henry Hwang, Banana Yoshimoto.
Jar of Dreams —Yoshiko Uchida
Dragonwings, The Lost Garden, The Star Fisher, Tongues of Jade,
   Dragon's Gate, Child of the Owl, The Rainbow People, American Dragons
   —Lawrence Yep
Farewell to Manzanar—James D. Houston & Jeanne Wakatsuki Houston
Children of the River—Linda Crew
Vatsana's Lucky New Year—Sara Gogol
The Moved-Outers—Florence Means
My Name is San Ho —Jayne Pettit
The Japanese in America—Noel Leathers
Tales from Gold Mountain: Stories of the Chinese in the New World—Paul Yee
In the Year of the Boar and Jackie Robinson—Betty Bao Lord

For high-level readers:

Short stories by Banana Yoshimoto, Maxine Hong Kingston, Amy Tan
To Stand Against the Wind—Ann Nolan Clark
Angel Child, Dragon Child—Michele Surat
The Absolutely Perfect Horse —Marylois Dunn
American Eyes (short stories edited by Lori M. Carlson)
Kim/Kimi—Hadley Irwin
Famous Asian Americans—Janet Nomura Morey and Wendy Dunn

Other Literature about the Immigrant Experience:

Out of this Furnace by Thomas Bell (three generations of Slovakian immigrants); *A
Good Scent from a Strange Mountain* (Vietnamese); *Seventeen Syllables and Other Stories*
(interned Japanese); *My Antonia* by Willa Cather; *The Education of Hyman Kaplan* by
Leonard Q. Ross; *And the Earth Did Not Swallow Him* by Tomas Rivera; *A Bridge Between
Us* by Julie Shigekuni; *When Heaven and Earth Changed Places: A Vietnamese Woman's
Journey from War to Peace* by Le Ly Hayslip; *Barrio Boy* by Ernesto Galarza; *Woman
Hollering Creek and Other Stories* by Sandra Cisneros; *Imagining America: Stories from
the Promised Land: A Multicultural Anthology of American Fiction* edited by Wesley
Brown and Amy Ling; *No-No Boy* by John Okada (Japanese)

Internet Sites

Search for *The Joy Luck Club* and you will find a summary of the movie, movie trivia and reviews of the movie by Roger Ebert and others. Click on:

http://us.imdb.com/M/multi-search

For an interesting contrast to all the positive reviews, look at the objections one Asian American has to what he sees as the negative stereotyping in the movie. Click on:

http://www.cs.indiana.edu/hyplan/tanaka/disparity/Jlc.txt

Research

Confucianism:

Fingarette, Herbert. *Confucius—The Secular as Sacred.* New York: Harper & Row, 1972.

Taoism:

Mitchell, Steven. *Tao Te Ching.* New York: Harper & Row, 1988.
Yutang, Lin. *The Wisdom of Lao Tzu.* New York: Modern Library, 1976.

Writing Activities

1. **Essay Topics**
    *   How does Amy Tan weave elements of Taoism, Confucianism, and Buddhism throughout these sixteen stories?
    *   Compare and contrast the four daughters.
    *   Compare and contrast the four mothers.
    *   Using *Bartlett's Familiar Quotations* or a similar reference book, find a famous quote that somehow ties in with the story. Explain the connection.
    *   Choose one of the mothers and explore what she values most. How has she attempted to transmit these values to her daughter?
    *   Trace images of the Chinese mother tradition throughout the book.
    *   Compare and contrast June with another character from another story who experiences "culture clash" (See Related Reading, above, for suggested comparison readings.)
    *   Write an essay that begins with this quote by Alice Walker: "Amy Tan shows us China, Chinese-American women and their families, and the mystery of the mother-daughter bond in ways that we have not experienced before."

- Analyze the main types of conflict that drive these stories. Cite examples of "Person vs. Person," "Person vs. Society," and "Inner Conflict."
- Discuss the italicized tales that begin each section. How does each set the tone and theme for the section it precedes?
- What is Amy Tan saying about family bonds and the tradition of children — especially daughters—honoring their mothers?
- What is Amy Tan saying about immigration and cultural tradition?
- What is Amy Tan saying about freedom of choice?

2. Assume the persona of one of the women in the book. Write several entries in your private diary, from several points in time.

3. Assume the persona of one of these women's therapists. Write notes summarizing three of your sessions—your observations and recommendations.

4. Write a poem in response to the novel. For example:
   - a diamente that describes how June changes
   - a prayer poem by An-mei
   - a love poem by Rich
   - a bitterness poem by Rose
   - a list poem by Lena
   - a poem that ends with a line taken from the story
   - a once/now poem about changing traditions in the story

5. Write two or three items of relevance to the story that might appear in the *San Francisco Chronicle* (e.g., Suyuan Woo's obituary; Waverly and Rich's marriage announcement; an ad in the job section of the classified to which June might respond; a news article about the polio epidemic when the girls were small).

6. Write a letter of advice to Rose about how to get over—or get back at—Ted.

7. Describe a dream that June has when she falls asleep on the plane on the way home from China.

8. Write a "Dear Abby" letter from June's point of view.

9. Write a "Can This Marriage Be Saved?" article for a women's magazine that focuses on Harold and Lena.

10. Write a letter to Amy Tan in which you react to her book—and ask her at least one thoughtful question about it.

Listening/Speaking

1. **Video:** Watch the movie and compare/contrast it with the book. What do you think of the casting? Are the characters as you imagined them? How has the book's shifting point of view been handled in the movie? What changes and deletions do you note? What is your impression of the cinematography? Would you recommend the movie to a friend?

2. **Debate:** Debate some of the opinions expressed in the novel. For instance:
   It is best to swallow your tears.
   Some secrets should be kept from children.
   You shouldn't listen to too many people.

3. **Interview:** Stage a TV talk show (à la Oprah Winfrey) about mothers and daughters. Eight students act out the parts of the four mothers and daughters; the other students ask questions. ("Actresses" should "absorb their roles" by rereading pertinent sections of the book the night before; "audience members" should compose questions for homework.)

4. Break into several small groups and act out some of the stories in *The Joy Luck Club.*

5. Write a scene that is mentioned but not described in the book (e.g., Rose Hsu's wedding).

6. Write a scene that does not happen in the book—but might have. For example, what sort of "send-off" did the relatives give June and her father at the airport?

Language Study

1. Create a glossary of the Chinese words and phrases you find in the story.

2. Find out which Chinese cities have undergone name changes during the last 50 years—and why.

3. June's father speaks a Mandarin dialect, but the rest of the family speaks Cantonese. Find out more about the various Chinese dialects and how they arose.

4. Amy Tan uses a great deal of figurative language. Make a list of the metaphors, similes, and allusions you find in her stories and analyze what makes them effective.

Art

1. Choose one of the mother-daughter pairs in this book and create a collage that captures your impressions of them.

2. Create a mobile of objects from the book (e.g., mah jong tile, piano music, chess piece, etc.). Label each with a brief description of the role it plays in *The Joy Luck Club.*

3. Choose your favorite story from the collection. Summarize it in the form of a five-frame cartoon-strip.

4. Several dreams are described in these stories. Choose one and illustrate it, using chalk on wet paper.

5. Learn about the artwork that the mothers might have seen when they were young girls in China, before World War II.

6. Illustrate one of the settings described in the story, e.g., the Hsus' living room, the courtyard on the day of the Moon Festival, Harold and Lena's kitchen, etc.

7. Pretend that you are one of the daughters. Create a Mother's Day card for your mother. Include a one-paragraph note to your mother.

Music

1. Small group project: Choose one of the stories from *Joy Luck Club* that is set in China, pre-1949. Select music that would be appropriate as background music and tape your reading of that story.

2. Listen to the piece Jing-mei played at the recital—and its companion (Schumann's "Pleading Child" and "Perfectly Contented") as well as other pieces mentioned in the story (like "The Flight of the Bumblebee," which Jing-mei's father was humming).

Science

1. June's father says that his wife died from an idea that grew too big and burst. Research the actual causes, effects, and treatments for a brain aneurysm.

2. Find out more about the polio epidemic that occurred when the daughters were young.

3. Write a short research report on anorexia. Include a list of places you could contact if you were trying to find help for someone with an eating disorder.

History/Current Events

1. Find out more about the history of concubines—and the ongoing debate about them. For example, it is estimated that in 1997 there will be 240,000 children born in China to concubines of men from Hong Kong. For an interesting presentation of different viewpoints, click on:
   http://www.cuhk.hic/journal/varsity/9504/concub.htm
   What do you think An-mei Hsu's viewpoint on the issue would be?

2. Learn more about what it was like to live in mainland China during the years prior to 1949—particularly, what it was like for women. There are several informative sites on the Internet. Start with "Awesome China Links" at:
   http://www.lgcy.com/skyway/links/AADHchin.htm

3. Find out more about the Moon Festival described in the fourth story. (For those in the Milwaukee area, find out more about the Asian Moon Festival.)

4. June and her father enter China after leaving Hong Kong. Find out about the current status of relations between these two areas.

5. Find out more about Taoism, Confucianism, and Buddhism—three philosophies whose elements appear in *The Joy Luck Club.* For an interesting essay by Peter Tavernise on how these sacred systems are woven into the fabric of the novel, click on: **http://www.duke.edu//~ptavern/Pete.Tan.html**

6. Research China during the years before and during World War II. Find out more about Sun Yat-sen, Chiang Kai-shek, Nationalism, Communism, the changing status of Taiwan and Hong Kong. (An excellent website: **http://www.grolier.com.** Click on "interactive World War II commemoration; then go to —"The War in Eastern Asia.")

Geography

1. Create a map showing locations important to the story in both China and the
    U.S. Label each location with a brief explanation of how it figures in the story.
    Include: Shanghai, Kweilin (now Guilin), Chungking (now Chongqing),
    Shenzhen, Canton (now Guangzhou). Also include these California locations:
    San Francisco, Oakland, Berkeley. (There are several maps available on the
    Internet. You might start with the small map of China (CIA) at:

    http://darkwing.uoregon.edu/~felsing/cstuff/chinamap.html

    and the detailed map of China at
    http://www.lib.utexas.edu/Libs/PCL/Map_collection/middle_east_

    and
    _asia/China.GIF

    and the California map at:
    http://www.gowest.com/maps/calif/state/basic/calif.htm

2. Pretend that you are writing the guidebook June takes on her trip to China.
    Include entries that describe the places she visits: Shenzhen, Guangzhou,
    Shanghai. Include two other cities in China you would highly recommend. (A
    good source of information about history and offerings of various cities is the
    China Pages at **http://www.china-pages/com/culture**. You can also get there
    from "Awesome China Links"—see above.)

Culinary

1. Try making some of the foods mentioned in the story, e.g., Auntie Lin's red
    bean soup, Suyuan Woo's black sesame-seed soup, the moon cake little Ying-
    ying ate at the Moon Festival, or the spicy bean curd dish June makes for her
    father. There are many recipes on the Internet. You might want to start with
    one of the pages of Chinese recipes, such as:
    http://www.cs.cmu.edu/mjw/recipes/ethnic/chinese/chinese.html

2. Kitchens and eating are recurrent motifs throughout Amy Tan's stories. For an
    interesting essay on Chinese cooking (history, regional styles, kitchen culture,
    etc.), click on:
    http://www.halcyon.com/thoskite/kitchens.htm

Assessment for *The Joy Luck Club*

Assessment should be a continuous process—more than a quiz at the end of the book. Below is a chart to facilitate on-going portfolio assessment. Students should check off items on the list below as they complete them. Points for each project successfully completed may be placed in the "Teacher" column to show the level of achievement.

Name ______________________________   Date__________________________

Student   Teacher

_______ _______   1.   As you read, keep a Response Log. (See pages 6-7 for some suggested formats.)

_______ _______   2.   Create a map showing China and California. Show the journeys taken by the four mothers to the U.S. and the trip June and her father take in the end.

_______ _______   3.   Participate in a classroom debate about one of the statements in Initiating Activity #2, page 5.

_______ _______   4.   Write a short-story sequel to *The Joy Luck Club* told from a male character's point of view.

_______ _______   5.   Draw an illustration to accompany the passage that you found most striking in Tan's novel.

_______ _______   6.   Compile the scrapbook that one of the mothers might have kept, with a caption for each item.

_______ _______   7.   Create a poster of newspaper pieces that somehow relate to *The Joy Luck Club,* and caption each with a brief explanation of the link.

_______ _______   8.   Write a poem about one of the mother-daughter pairs in the book.

_______ _______   9.   Small group activity: Participate in acting out one of the stories.

_______ _______   10. After reading the novel, write an essay using one of the topics on pages 38-40.

_______ _______   11. Alternative activity of your choice:

_______ _______   12. Write a self-evaluation of your portfolio, explaining the strengths and weaknesses of various pieces and assigning yourself an overall grade.

Note: For quizzes, tests, a study guide, and activity sheets focusing on critical thinking skills, vocabulary study, literary analysis, and writing skills, see the **Novel Units Student Packet** for *The Joy Luck Club.*